THE FIRST WORLD WAR

SCOTTISH RECORD OFFICE

EDINBURGH

HER MAJESTY'S STATIONERY OFFICE

ISBN 0 11 493339 1

ACKNOWLEDGEMENTS

CONTENTS

The Scottish Record Office is grateful to the following owners for permission to use documents in their collections, The Right Honourable The Earl of Airlie, Miss M. Anderson, Edinburgh, Sir Ilay M. Campbell, Bt., Sir John Clerk of Penicuik, Bt., Sir Archibald Grant of Monymusk, Bt., Sir Archibald P. Hope of Craighall, Bt., The Most Honourable The Marquess of Lothian, The Right Honourable The Earl of Mar and Kellie, Mr A.M.H. Matheson, Brahan, Conon Bridge, United Biscuits Ltd, and Miss E. Walker, Edinburgh. Thanks are also due to the following owners of copyright for permission to reproduce and quote from letters, Miss Joan Allen, London (the letter from her father, Baron Allen of Hurtwood), The Right Honourable the Earl of Mar and Kellie (that from the Countess of Mar and Kellie to Lord Erskine), Brigadier H.L.B. Salmon (those of his great-aunt, Miss Sarah Macnaughtan), Mr D. Thomson, Warwick (those of his father, the Rev. R.J. Thomson), and Miss A.C. Victor, Edinburgh (her own letter to Lady Clementine Waring).

Thanks are due for the use of photographs to the Chief Librarian, Edinburgh City Libraries, *The Illustrated London News,* from which photographs were copied by Mr A.M. Broom of the Scottish Record Office, and the Trustees of the Imperial War Museum, London.

Compiled by Dr Margaret H.B. Sanderson
Exhibitions and Education Officer
Scottish Record Office.

INTRODUCTION

The First World War and its effect on the lives of those who fought in and lived through it can be recalled in a number of ways; in written, printed and visual records, oral and other sound-archives and film, in the weapons and other relics of the war and at those places associated with the military conflict itself.

This Archive Unit, drawn from the wide-ranging holdings of the Scottish Record Office, tries to recreate a picture of the war years through a variety of contemporary records, public and private, official and personal. The documents have been chosen not simply for their factual content (for there are many books about the War) but because they convey a variety of attitudes of the time towards the war itself: early patriotic enthusiasm; first-hand accounts of conditions in the trenches on both the Western and Eastern Fronts and in the camps; the work of nurses behind the lines; reaction to the unprecedented loss of life in battle in modern times; the new experience at home of wartime austerity; the atmosphere of fear and suspicion in the community; women in war work; criticism of the conduct of the war, pacifist attitudes and the case of conscientious objectors; government control of work, food-supplies and transport during the emergency; the role of the press in keeping up morale.

The aim has been to let the documents speak for themselves but explanatory notes, commentary and introductory passages to the main themes are provided. In addition there are quotations from letters and documents which are not actually reproduced in the Unit. Scottish Record Office references and attributions of photographs are given. Much of the material appears in print for the first time thanks to the kind permission of those whose names are given in the Acknowledgements.

An extensive 'Source List of documents in the Scottish Record Office relating to military matters', including the First and Second World Wars, is available in the Office's Search Rooms where the records themselves may be consulted, Monday-Friday, 9.00-4.45. A selection of free Information Leaflets on the holdings and facilities of the Scottish Record Office, including services for schools, will be sent on request. All enquiries about the above Source List or about this Archive Unit should be addressed to

The Scottish Record Office
HM General Register House
Princes Street
Edinburgh EH1 3YY
Tel: 031-556 6585.

1 THE PATH OF DUTY

The wave of patriotic enthusiasm that swept the country on the outbreak of war brought queues of men from all walks of life to the recruiting offices as the Government, under the direction of Lord Kitchener, the War Secretary, launched a massive recruiting campaign accompanied by posters which have become some of the best-known 'documents' of the war.

DON'T IMAGINE YOU ARE NOT WANTED

EVERY MAN between 19 and 38 years of age is WANTED! Ex-Soldiers up to 45 years of age

"YOUR COUNTRY NEEDS YOU"

MEN CAN ENLIST IN THE NEW ARMY FOR THE DURATION OF THE WAR

RATE OF PAY: Lowest Scale 7s. per week with Food, Clothing &c., in addition

1. Separation Allowance for Wives and Children of Married Men when separated from their Families (Inclusive of the allotment required from the Soldier's pay of a maximum of 6d. a day in the case of a private)

For a Wife **without** Children	-	12s. 6d. per week
For Wife with One Child	-	15s. 0d. per week
For Wife with Two Children	-	17s. 6d. per week
For Wife with Three Children	-	20s. 0d. per week
For Wife with Four Children	-	22s. 0d per week

and so on, with an addition of **2s.** for each additional child.
Motherless children 3s. a week each, exclusive of allotment from Soldier's pay

2. Separation Allowance for Dependants of Unmarried Men.

Provided the Soldier does his share, the Government will assist liberally in keeping up, within the limits of Separation Allowance for Families, any regular contribution made before enlistment by unmarried Soldiers or Widowers to other dependants such as mothers, fathers, sisters, etc.

YOUR COUNTRY IS STILL CALLING. FIGHTING MEN! FALL IN!!

Full Particulars can be obtained at any Recruiting Office or Post Office.

1 One of the famous Kitchener posters which were displayed all over the country on every available space.

The British Government, having declared war on Germany on 4 August 1914, on the latter's invasion of Belgium, issued determined statements which echoed popular patriotism:

'We shall never sheathe the sword which we have not lightly drawn until Belgium recovers in full measure all and more than all that she has sacrificed, until France is adequately secured against the menace of aggression, until the rights of the smaller nationalities of Europe are placed upon an unassailable foundation, and until the military domination of Prussia is wholly and finally destroyed' — Mr Asquith, Prime Minister, 9 November 1914.

LOTHIAN MUNIMENTS: GD 40/17/671/5

November, 1914.

Young Men, Your Country Needs You !

MORE men are urgently required for the Regular Army. They are required NOW. It is of no use sending untrained men into the field. If you want to help your country at this critical moment, you must come forward NOW, and be trained as a soldier.

You will not be sent to the front till you are trained and fit to take the field against the enemy. As soon as you are trained you will be given your chance to show the stuff that is in you.

You are not asked to join the Army in the ordinary way, which involves service in peace time, though you will be welcome if you do so. You are only asked to serve for the War. As soon as the War is over, every facility will be given you to secure your discharge, and get back to your ordinary work.

Kitchener

WAR OFFICE, WHITEHALL.

Published by the PARLIAMENTARY RECRUITING COMMITTEE, 12, Downing St., London, S.W., and Printed by HAZELL, WATSON & VINEY, LD., 52, Long Acre, London, W.C.

Leaflet No. 17.

W 8004—128   100,000   11/14

2 A War Office leaflet of November 1914 calling for recruits for the regular army for the duration of the war; many people hoped it would all be over in a few months — even by Christmas.

GOVERNMENT LEAFLET

3 A queue at a recruiting office. By the beginning of 1915 the number of recruits was over one million.

4 Information on recruitment was available at all Post Offices and the many recruiting offices, bringing the thought of war nearer many families in rural areas. This notice was printed, for local information, at Kirriemuir, Angus.

AIRLIE MUNIMENTS: GD 16/52/60

ANY ONE WHO IS OVER 19 AND NOT OVER 35 CAN ENLIST.
SO CAN ALL EX-SOLDIERS UP TO 45.

Men will naturally ask:

1. "For how long shall I have to serve?"

   Answer: Till the end of the War and no longer. The men of the Second Army will be first to be discharged when Peace comes.

2. "What will happen to my Wife and Children?"

   Answer: Your wife will get 1s 1d a day separation allowance for herself and 2d for each child. If that is not enough to keep the home together, she can look with perfect confidence to the Village or the Town, the County, and the Nation to do what is needful.

3. "What pay shall I get for myself?"

   Answer: You will get, to begin with, 1s 3d a day and all found and well found.

4. "What will happen to me if I am maimed by the loss of a limb?"

   Answer: You will receive a pension, as every regular soldier does in similar circumstances.

A trained soldier is what Britain wants, and you will be well trained before you are sent abroad.

Apply at the nearest Recruiting Office or any Post Office.

Printed by J. NORRIE, "Free Press" Office, Kirriemuir.

5 Troop movements around the country towards depots and embarkation points, using the railway network, also brought the idea of war nearer home. Pride in the local effort is written across this postcard, showing soldiers and horses at Moniaive Station, Dumfriesshire, 1914:

'Should think Salisbury would be jealous of Moniaive now. Good job the Kaiser will have difficulty in finding a map with this on it.'

6 Illustrations from *The Complete Patrol*, written by 'An Expert' for the instruction of officers in '2/1 Regiment of Blankshire Crashers'. The soldiers' capacity for looking on the lighter side of their duties became legendary.

WARING OF LENNEL PAPERS: GD 372/303

"Choose your men. Mainly so that each section gets the same chance of being shot"

Information. *"Remember that information which may appear of little or no importance to you may be of <u>infinite</u> value when placed in the hands of the proper authorities."*

7 The equipment carried to the Front by the British soldier in the First World War: 'the best-equipped and best-fed fighting-man in the world'. By the winter of 1914-15 the soldier carried 66lbs (30Kg) weight of equipment.

THE ILLUSTRATED LONDON NEWS, 27 FEBRUARY 1915:
BRITISH RAILWAYS RECORDS: BR/PER(S)34/113

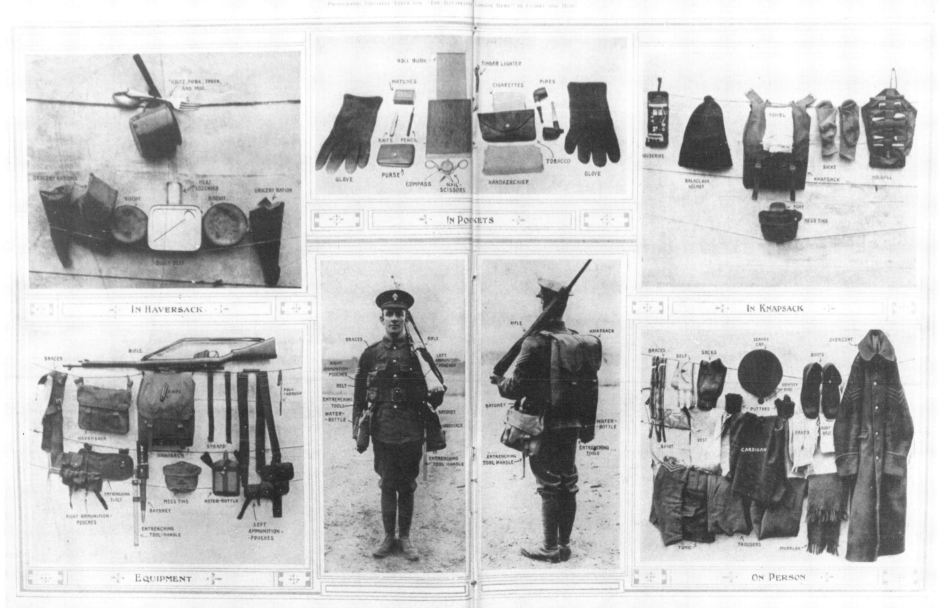

GUARANTEEING EFFICIENCY AND COMFORT: WHAT THE BRITISH SOLDIER BEARS TO THE FIRING-LINE.

IN HAVERSACK: IN POCKETS: IN KNAPSACK: ON PERSON: AND EQUIPMENT: THE BURDEN CARRIED BY "TOMMY" WHEN MARCHING TO THE TRENCHES.

2 FLANDERS AND THE DARDANELLES: 1914-15

A comparatively small but efficient force of 100,000 men — the British Expeditionary Force — was mobilised and landed in France within a week of the declaration of war. Nicknamed the 'Old Contemptibles' after the Kaiser had referred to them as General French's 'contemptible little army', the B.E.F. were the first British troops to bear the brunt of the fighting in the early battles on the Western Front, Mons, Marne and Ypres. By the end of 1915 their casualties were being replaced by the trained recruits of 'Kitchener's New Armies'.

8 Troops of the B.E.F. sailing for France in August 1914. Those in the photograph are from the Royal Scots (in flat caps) and the Gordon Highlanders (in glengarrys).

Although a naval arms-race between Britain and Germany had preceded the outbreak of hostilities there were few major naval actions in the first two years of the war. An exception was that off Heligoland Bight in August 1914 when, under the command of Admiral Beatty, the British fleet destroyed four German vessels. The main value of the British navy was in protecting the transportation of troops to France, and the food supply routes to Britain, while building up a blockade of Germany's maritime trade.

9 A letter to Lord Erskine, serving in France, from his mother on the death of a 15-year old nephew in the sinking of the *Aboukir* off the coast of the Netherlands on 22 September 1914.

'Of course one is proud of him but oh! it is desperately young to be called upon to give one's life for one's country'.

Details of the circumstances followed shortly afterwards:

'Evidently they had all been very sea sick three days before they were torpedoed . . . the fearful cold of the water may have numbed him at once and exhausted him . . . It is wicked to have sent those children into that fearful strain. They were doing patrol work all the time in the North Sea and had sent their destroyers into port on account of the bad weather and should never have been cruising about without them. Those slow old boats are absolutely defenceless.'

MAR AND KELLIE MUNIMENTS: GD 124/15/1852/1-2

10 For the wounded soldier, and over half the troops received a wound of some kind, it was a painful process reaching the field hospital — the slow progress through the mud by the stretcher party to the regimental Aid-Post for initial treatment, then to the Advanced Dressing Station and on to the Casualty Clearing Station, where most surgery was done, hot food was available and the civilising sight of nurses helped to blot out the nightmare of the trenches, however temporarily. Nurses, who arrived in France in ever-increasing numbers, were not allowed nearer the front than the Casualty Clearing Stations but, as this letter from Miss Sarah Macnaughtan shows, that did not rule out being near the enemy. Having described the problem of feeding the wounded she concluded (passage not shown):

'Last night I was dressing wounds and bandaging in Dunkirk Station till 3 a.m. The men are brought there in heaps, all helpless, all suffering, sometimes there are fifteen hundred in one day. Last night seven hundred lay on straw in a huge Railway shed, with straw to cover them, bedded down like cattle and all in pain. Still it's better than the trenches and shrapnel overhead. At the field Hospital the wounds were ghastly and we are losing so many patients. Mere boys of sixteen come in sometimes mortally wounded and there are a good many cases of wounded women. You see, no one is safe. Have you ever seen a Town that has been thoroughly shelled?'

WARING OF LENNEL PAPERS: GD 372/93/3

11 Part of a letter to his English-speaking wife from a German officer, in 1914, describing the difficulties of finding fresh food and keeping clean in camp:

'I don't know if I told you that before leaving Aachen I bought a big india rubber folding bath. It is a great boon, as I never need want a bath even in Bivuak, and am as yet quite clean . . . Only the stomach revolts now and again at the sights and smells. There is really nothing more revolting than a deserted station, filled with wounded and smelling of carbol, cooking and thrown away meats . . . but our men are in a very good state of health and have never hungered'.

COLLECTION OF DUNDAS AND WILSON, C.S., DAVIDSON AND SYME, W.S.: GD 282/13/314

12 This photograph is said to show an actual attack by the Germans on a British position, near Ypres, 1915. Few photographs of the conflict appeared in British newspapers early in the war and reports tended to minimise losses by the Allies. This picture, like many others at that time, is believed to be posed. In the first battle of Ypres (called Wipers by the British troops) the British suffered about 50,000 casualties but prevented a German breakthrough to the Channel ports.

THE ILLUSTRATED LONDON NEWS, 5 JUNE 1915: BRITISH RAILWAYS RECORDS: BR/PER(S)34/113

During the trench warfare soldiers frequently risked their lives by running out into the 'no man's land' between the trenches to bring in wounded comrades for aid or the dead for decent burial. Many bereaved families at home longed to know the circumstances of a soldier's death.

13 A soldier beside the body of a fallen comrade awaiting burial.

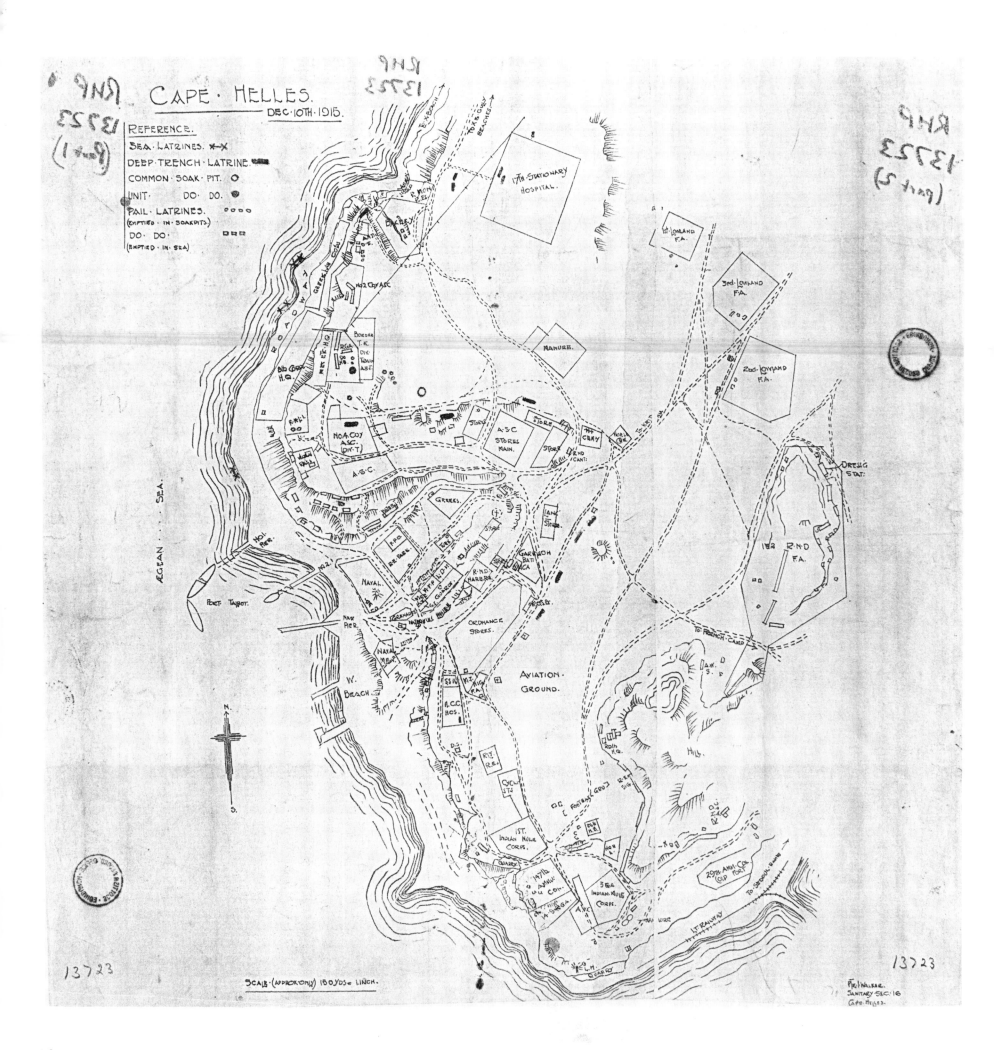

In the spring of 1915, in order to relieve pressure on Russia by opening up a supply route through the Black Sea, and in an attempt to knock Turkey, an ally of the Central Powers, out of the war, the Allies attacked Turkish positions in the Dardanelles, the first channel in the waterway linking the Mediterranean with the Black Sea. An initial naval attack having failed, a combined force of British, Australian and New Zealand troops was landed on the Gallipoli peninsula. The operation was badly planned and carried out, the Turks had early warning of the landings and a situation developed like that on the Western Front with the soldiers digging themselves in for trench warfare, in scorching summer temperatures.

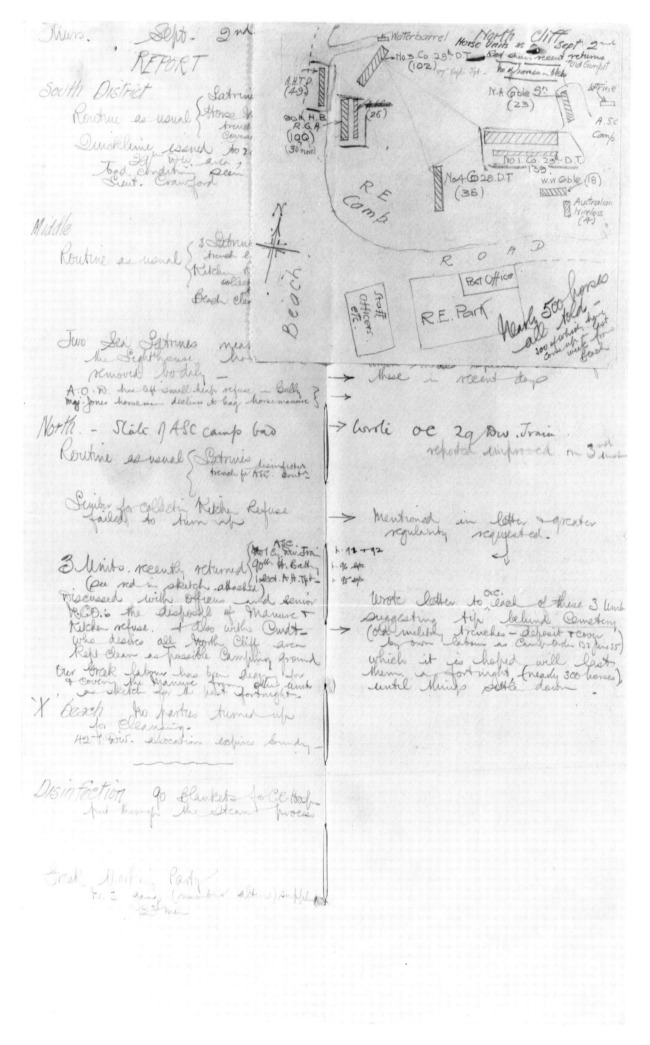

14 Map showing the camp at Cape Helles, Dardanelles, 10 December 1915; from the papers of Lt. John Crawford of the Royal Army Medical Corps.

REGISTER HOUSE PLANS: RHP 13/723

15 Pages of the Field Hospital Book of Lt. John Crawford, R.A.M.C., Dardanelles campaign. His notes highlight the problems of a medical officer in the insanitary conditions of the camp:

'Two Sea Latrines near the Lighthouse have been removed bodily; Limber [part of a gun-carriage] for collecting Kitchen Refuse failed to turn up; 'X' Beach, no parties turned up for cleaning; Disinfection, 90 blankets for C.C. Hospital put through the steam process; Nearly 500 horses all told, 300 of which have come up in last week from the Beach; Maj. Jones horseman declines to bag horsemanure.'

COLLECTION OF MORTON, FRASER AND MILLIGAN, W.S.: GD 232/16/3

16 The Eastern Front: French and British troops at Salonika, Greece, where some of those evacuated from the Dardanelles were sent to strengthen the Allied garrison against Bulgaria. Trapped in this position without having much effect on the Balkans situation, they were referred to by the Kaiser as his 'largest prisoner of war camp'.

3 THE HOME FRONT

The First World War affected British families in a way that previous wars had not, to the extent that people felt they were fighting on a 'home front'. There were soon food shortages and increased prices, especially on imported foodstuffs. A drive to produce home-grown food turned many public and private gardens, as well as many previously uncultivated areas, into vegetable plots. Under the Defence of the Realm Act of 8 August 1914 the government assumed direct control of certain resources and communications vital to the war-effort, such as railways, docks and harbours. With the threat of air-raids and the possible approach of enemy shipping the use of lighting was restricted after dark. People were encouraged to be on the look-out for 'spies' and warned not to spread any information that might be of use to the enemy. In the interest of the war-effort the government had power to move workers from less important to priority jobs, while thousands of women moved into work previously done by men who had gone off to fight. Some of this work was tough and included the new, vital work in munitions factories.

17 Statutory rules and orders on lighting restrictions, 1916, drawn up under the Defence of the Realm Act (usually referred to as DORA).

RECORDS OF THE SCOTTISH HOME AND HEALTH DEPARTMENT: HH 31/21

FOR OFFICIAL USE.

STATUTORY RULES AND ORDERS, 1916.

No. $\frac{65}{S.3}$.

DEFENCE OF THE REALM.

THE LIGHTS (SCOTLAND) (No. 1) ORDER OF 9TH FEBRUARY, 1916, MADE BY THE SECRETARY FOR SCOTLAND UNDER REGULATION 11 OF THE DEFENCE OF THE REALM (CONSOLIDATION) REGULATIONS, 1914.

In pursuance of the power conferred on me by Regulation 11 of the Defence of the Realm (Consolidation) Regulations, 1914, I hereby make the following Order:—

(1) All lights, whether public or private, which, if unobscured, would be visible from the sea or from the navigable waters of any estuary, must be extinguished, or, in the case of indoor lights, obscured so as to be invisible from outside:

Provided that this paragraph shall not apply to lights on vehicles, or to indispensable navigation, railway or dock lights, or to lights in shipbuilding yards, armament works and other factories which are excepted under paragraph (5) below, or to any light which is approved by a competent naval or military authority.

(2) Subject to the later provisions of this Order, all external lamps, flares and fixed lights of all descriptions, and all aggregations of lights, whether public or private, must be extinguished, except such public lamps as in the opinion of the Chief Constable are necessary for safety and any other lights approved by him.

All lights which are not extinguished must be reduced to the minimum intensity consistent with safety and shaded or obscured so as to render them invisible from above and to cut off direct light in all directions above the horizontal.

(3) The intensity of the inside lighting of shops and shop fronts must be reduced or the lights obscured or shaded so that no more than a dull subdued light is visible outside and no part of the pavement or roadway or any building is distinctly illuminated thereby: in particular, all sources of light must be shaded with some opaque material so that all direct light therefrom is cut off from the windows and doors.

(4) In hotels, flats, dwelling houses and premises of all descriptions not coming under other provisions of this Order, inside lights must be so shaded or reduced or the windows, skylights and glass doors so screened by shutters or dark blinds or curtains, &c., that no more than a dull subdued light is visible from any direction outside.

[Price 1d.]

(1200—15.) Wt. 151—599. 3000. 2/16. D & S. G. 10.

2

(5) In factories, workshops and other such buildings which are illuminated at night the roof areas and windows must be covered over or obscured and the lighting intensity reduced to the minimum necessary for the safe and expeditious progress of work:

Provided that lighting may be maintained in shipbuilding yards, armament works and other factories engaged in the manufacture of articles required for the fulfilment of Government contracts, to such extent as may be necessary for the safe and expeditious progress of work.

(6) The intensity of the lighting of railway stations, sidings, goods yards, docks, &c. must be reduced to the minimum that will suffice for the safe and expeditious progress of work: the tops and sides of all external lights which cannot be dispensed with must be shaded or painted over.

(7) Passengers in railway carriages which are provided with blinds must keep the blinds lowered so as to cover the windows. The blinds may be lifted in case of necessity when the train is at a standstill at a station, but if lifted they must be lowered again before the train starts.

(8) With regard to lights on vehicles, the provisions of the Lights on Vehicles (Scotland) Order of 9th February, 1916 (Statutory Rules and Orders No. $\frac{67}{S.5}$), shall apply.

(9) In case of sudden emergency, all instructions as to the further reduction or extinction of lights given by or under the direction of a competent naval or military authority or the Chief Constable shall be immediately obeyed.

This Order shall take effect on and after 25th February, 1916, and shall apply to the period from half an hour after sunset till half an hour before sunrise.

The Order shall apply to the parishes named in the annexed Schedule and to that part of Scotland which lies to the south of a line passing from the coast of Aberdeenshire to the west coast of Argyllshire through the said parishes.

I hereby revoke, as from 25th February, 1916, Paragraph I. of the Order of the 8th April, 1915, as to lights in places on the coast of Scotland so far as applying to places to which this Order applies, without prejudice, however, to any proceedings in respect of contraventions of that Order.

This Order may be cited as the Lights (Scotland) (No. 1) Order of 9th February, 1916.

(L.S.)   T. McKinnon Wood,
                His Majesty's Secretary for
                    Scotland.

Scottish Office, Whitehall,
        9th February, 1916.

18 In April 1916 a Zeppelin raid was carried out over Edinburgh and Leith in which eight people, including three children, were killed. This photograph was taken in the Grassmarket, Edinburgh, after the raid.

THE EVENING DISPATCH, FRIDAY, APRIL 8, 1938

After the 1916 Zeppelin Raid

The scene in the Grassmarket twenty-two years ago after the first Zeppelins had raided Scotland and dropped bombs in various parts of Edinburgh

COUNTY OF MIDLOTHIAN.

NOTICE TO THE PUBLIC

IN THE EVENT OF

AN AERIAL RAID.

THE CHIEF-CONSTABLE ISSUES THE FOLLOWING INSTRUCTIONS FOR THE GUIDANCE OF HOUSE-HOLDERS IN THE COUNTY IN CASE OF AN AIR RAID :—

1. Immediately information is received that an Air Raid is imminent, the Gas—both Public and Private—will either be altogether cut off or be reduced to a minimum, and in those parts of the County where there is an Electric Installation, the Electric Light will be entirely cut off, and this should act as a warning that hostile aircraft is approaching or has begun an attack.

2. The Police at the same time will do their utmost to warn householders who use illuminants other than Gas or Electricity by informing them that an Air Raid is imminent, and this should be the signal for them to Extinguish all Inside Lights.

3. Householders using Gas are earnestly requested to extinguish what light remains, taking care to turn off the taps at the Gas Jets and Meter, to avoid danger in case of fire or of explosion or suffocation after the pressure is restored. Universal observance of this recommendation will produce the state of darkness which the Military Authorities consider so essential to public safety.

4. Householders, Shopkeepers, and others who are in the habit of keeping a small gas jet or jets burning overnight should discontinue the practice, as, with the gas reduced to a minimum in the event of an Air Raid, the light may go out, and on resumption of the pressure with open taps, the danger from suffocation and explosion is obvious.

5. The inhabitants are requested to remain Indoors during an Air Raid attack, keeping away from windows, and refraining from using lights of any kind. The danger of remaining outside is accentuated considerably by fragments of shells, &c., falling from our own defensive guns

6. Unexploded Shells or Bombs should on no account be interfered with, as they may burst when moved, but immediately it can be done with safety the Police should be informed of their position. By Regulation 35B of the Defence of the Realm Regulations it is an offence for any person having found any Bomb or Projectile or any Fragment thereof, or any Document, Map, &c., which may have been discharged, dropped, &c., from any hostile aircraft not to forthwith communicate the fact to a Military Post or to a Police Constable in the neighbourhood.

7. No matches must be struck nor lights of any description shown immediately before or during an Air Raid. The Lighting Restrictions must be strictly observed by the inhabitants. Darkness and silence are essential to public safety.

S. W. DOUGLAS, Major,
Chief-Constable.

20 Part of the report on a case of 'spies' at Dalwhinnie, Inverness-shire, who turned out to be Ordnance Survey personnel.

RECORDS OF THE SCOTTISH HOME AND HEALTH DEPARTMENT: HH 31/1

POLICE STATION,

NEWTONMORE, 18th. August, 1914.

Suspected persons at Dalwhinnie.

Sir,

JOHN CAMPBELL, (42) married, Merchant, residing at Farrow View, Dalwhinnie, Inverness-shire, states:-

On Monday, 17th. August, 1914 about 2 p.m. I saw a Motor Car standing on the Inverness and Perth public road at Dalwhinnie. In the Car were three men and a woman. About 3 p.m. I had occasion to go to Dalwhinnie Hotel, occupied by George Adams, Hotelkeeper, and while on my way there passed the same Car standing on the road midway between my shop and the Hotel. There was no person in the Car but I noticed that one of the men and the woman were about 80 yards off the road on the South side and near the bank of the River Truim. The man had a Theodolite mounted on a tripod, and was apparently taking a survey of the district on the south side of the River as the needle of the Theodolite was pointing southwards.

I passed on to the Hotel and on arriving there saw the other two men whom I had seen in the Car, in one of the Taprooms having a drink. I thought they looked rather suspicious and suggested to Mr. Adam that as they were on his ground he should ask them for their authority for acting as they were doing.

Mr. Adam challenged them in my hearing and one of the men said they were Government Surveyors. He then asked them to produce their credentials and the same man replied "I am sorry we forgot them, but "this should be sufficient", and he thereupon produced a telegram Form which he handed to Mr. Adam. I looked at the Form along with Mr. Adam and saw that the letters O.H.M.S. were printed on the top of it. Mr. Adam handed him back the form and he proceeded to write on it as if making out a telegraph message.

I then left the Hotel and returned to my house and again passed the man who was engaged surveying. On this occasion I saw that the/

2.

the needle of the Theodolite was pointing northwards in the direction of the Railway Line. I also noticed that he had what appeared to be a Camera on the ground beside him.

I noted the Index letters and Number of the Car which was C.F. 1. I then went away to Ben Alder on business and when I returned at 6 p.m. the Car and its occupants were gone.

Being suspicious of the movements of the party, in view of the present state of affairs, I thought it best to inform the Police of the matter and before going away to Ben Alder I wired Constable Campbell, Newtonmore informing him of the matter.

The following is a description of the persons referred to as near as I can give it, viz:-

No.1. About 40 years of age, 5 feet 4 or 5 inches in height, dark hair and moustache, otherwise shaved, thin build and stooping. Dressed in Grey tweed suit and light Overcoat or Waterproof.

No.2. Between 20 and 30 years of age, about 5 feet 8 or 9 inches in height, thinks clean shaved, and dressed in light grey clothes.

No.3. About 30 years of age, very short and stout, and dressed like a Chauffeur.

No.4. A woman, middle aged, very fair haired, height about 5 feet 1 or 2 inches. Dressed in Grey Coat.

Number 3 although dressed like a chauffeur appeared to be one of the party from the familiar way in which he was mixing with the others and it was he who paid for the drink while in the Hotel.

They spoke good English and I did not think they looked like foreigners.

21 A notice to workers, posted at an Ayrshire textile factory on the day war was declared. Six days later a 'Short Time Notice' appeared:

'We are having many orders cancelled and few coming in.

In order to spread the work over a longer period, we have decided to reduce the working hours per week.

On Thursday, and until further notice, work will begin at 9 o'clock a.m. and stop at 1. Saturdays 9 to 12.

We regret, under the very special circumstances, we shall be obliged to pay all classes of workers proportionately to these reduced hours, but any married man with a family, whose regular wage is 25/- [£1 25p] or less, is requested to report himself at the Office. Any such cases will be specially dealt with.*

We trust these very unusual conditions may have to last for a short time only.'

*Textile factories employed a very high proportion of female workers.

MORTON OF DARVEL PAPERS: GD 326/24/1

To Meet the New Conditions.

Aug 5th 1914

As employers, we shall keep things running as nearly as possible in their normal way, though it will doubtless be necessary to shorten the hours of labour.

May we advise our Workers in the times before us to keep cool and free from any sort of panic, and we can be of most service to our Country by observing a few simple rules at this juncture.

We should continue our life and habits as before, except that we should try to LIVE ON LESS.

On no account should we withdraw any monies we may have in Banks. We should draw out as little as/ever we can ever do with.

We should not lay in large stores of food and other necessaries. This only raises prices immediately against other people who cannot afford it, or who have the courage not to accumulate against their neighbours.

To rush for money and lay in large stores is most unpatriotic and un-neighbourly at this time. What is wanted in the present crisis is a feeling of " National Comradeship," where each will do all in his power to see the other through.

A. MORTON & CO.
MORTON SUNDOUR FABRICS, LTD.
HUDSON SCOTT & SONS, LTD.

WHY YOU SHOULD SAVE.

1. Save in every way possible for your Country's sake and for your own good.
2. Save for your Country's sake, because it is spending now £3,000,000 a day, and must find most of the money out of the savings of its citizens.
3. Save for your own sake, because while work and wages are good now, hard times may come after the War.
4. Save so that we need buy as little as possible from abroad. We are buying from foreign countries £1,000,000 a day more than they are buying from us.
5. Save, because whenever we import things that are not absolutely necessary it becomes more difficult to import and pay for all the things that are absolutely necessary.
6. Save, because the more we import from abroad the more difficult it is to prevent gold leaving the country in payment. Save, then, because our store of gold is vital to our credit and to our financial power.
7. Save, because by so doing you will help your Country to give financial help to our Allies who are less rich than we are.
8. **No saving is too small to count. If 45,000,000 people save an average of even half-a-crown a week, the total is huge—it means nearly £300,000,000 a year.**

How to Save.

1. Eat less meat.
2. Be careful with your bread.
3. Waste nothing. To waste food is as bad as to waste ammunition.
4. Save especially in all things which have to be imported; food and drink of all kinds, tobacco, petrol, rubber, etc.
5. Use home products wherever possible and be careful even with these.
6. Before you spend anything, think whether it is necessary.
7. If you possibly can, grow your own vegetables.

What You should do with your Savings.

1. Lend your savings to the Country to pay for the War and Victory.
2. If you have £5 to spare, go to the Post Office (Money Order Office), and buy a £5 Scrip Certificate.
   Keep this until December 1st, and then at any time before December 15th take it to the Post Office and exchange it for a £5 Stock Certificate. You will receive in addition 1/- bonus and also interest at the rate of 5d. for each complete month from the first day of the month after your purchase.
   You can buy as many of these Scrip Certificates as you are able, provided that the total amount purchased through the Post Office is not more than £200.
3. If you can spare only a few shillings, go to the Post Office and buy what is called a 5s. voucher. If you go on buying more 5s. vouchers until you have twenty, you can exchange them for a £5 stock certificate on December 1st, and you will then receive interest at the rate of a farthing for each full month on each voucher, from the first of the month after purchase until December 1st. In addition, when you convert your twenty vouchers into a £5 stock certificate you will get a bonus of 1s.

Leaflet No. 1.

[P.T.O.

The Departmental Committee on Food Production (Scotland) Report, of July 1915, revealed the different attitudes of people to the programme of turning over land to allotments in order to boost home-grown food supplies. Among those questioned was Mr James G. Robertson, organising secretary of the Scottish Farm Servants' Union.

'... I am not greatly in favour of smallholdings myself. I have been through the smallholdings and have seen the houses at Ballencrieff and other places, and I don't know if a man is to be much better off than he would be working on a big farm. The tools can never be the same; they are working with antiquated implements. I think the farm worker would rather have reasonable working conditions and a fairly decent wage working on a farm as he is now doing than be a smallholder ...

(Q) But there are several thousands of such men have applied for smallholdings.

(A) — But are they really farm servants? ... I was looking at a market garden place, some 18 acres, not far from Edinburgh, and the men that were working it did not know anything about farm work; ... A great many of the market gardeners have never been farm servants; they are rather men who are working at a hobby.'

RECORDS OF THE SCOTTISH HOME AND HEALTH DEPARTMENT: HH 31/24/1

We risk our lives to bring you food. It's up to you not to waste it.

J.P.Beadle.
1917

"A Message from our Seamen"

24 Photographs taken in Callander, Perth-shire, and Castle Douglas, Dumfriesshire, during the 'Tank Campaign' organised by local committees of the Scottish Savings Committee, set up as part of the National Savings Movement in May 1916. People were encouraged to save locally, and by purchasing either War Bonds or War Savings Certificates to 'buy' a war weapon, tank or aeroplane. Schoolchildren as well as adults received talks on the importance of saving in the war-effort, and the tanks — the great new weapon, first used by the British on the Somme in September 1916 — were 'paraded' through towns and villages.

RECORDS OF THE NATIONAL SAVINGS COMMITTEE: NSC 1/392/1

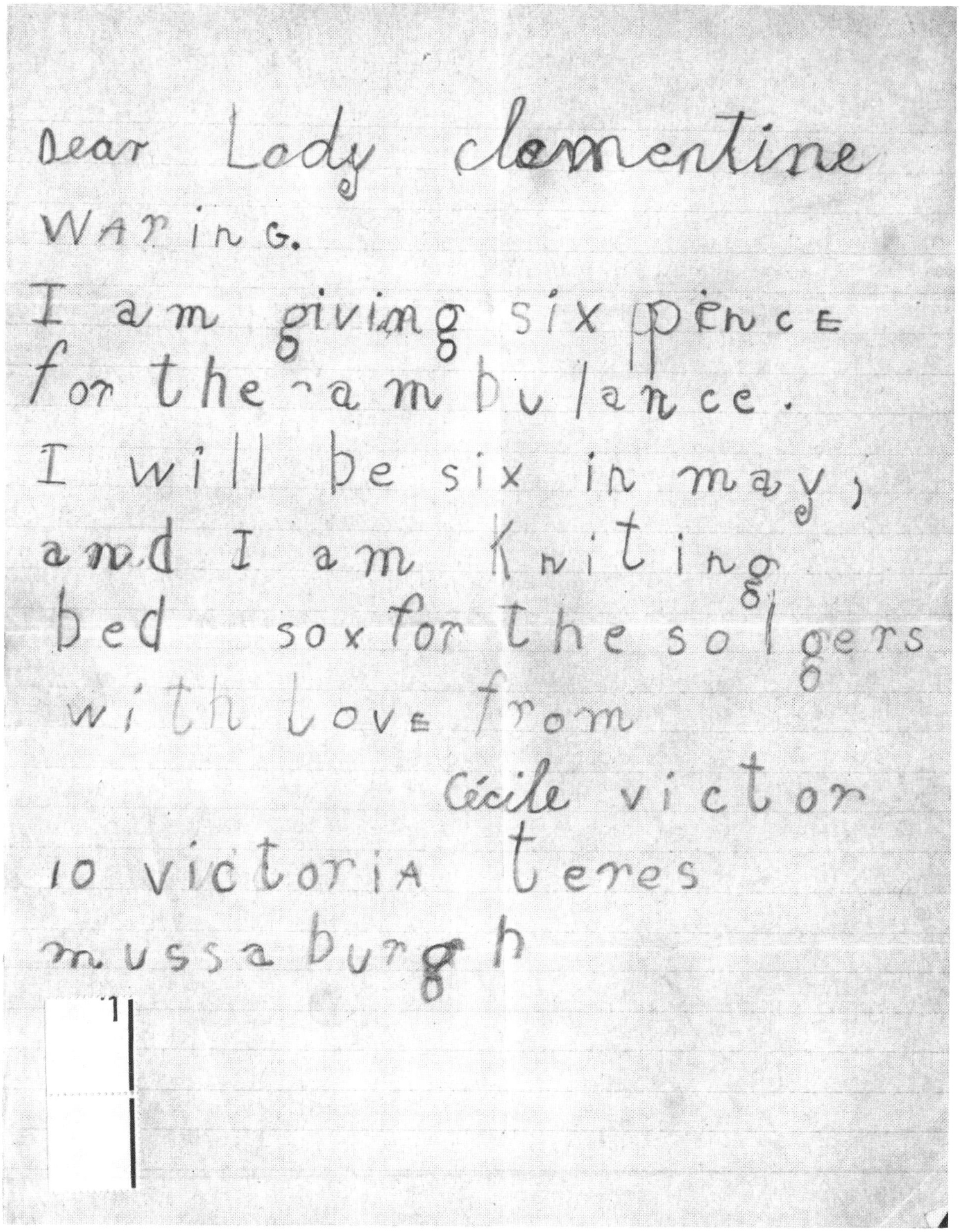

Dear Lady clementine Waring.

I am giving sixpence for the ambulance.

I will be six in may, and I am kniting bed sox for the solgers

with love from

Cécile victor

10 victoria teres mussaburgh

26 On the other side of the Channel the women of Rheims, which suffered heavy bombardments, were photographed knitting in the shelter of the wine vaults.

THE ILLUSTRATED LONDON NEWS, 9 JANUARY 1915:
BRITISH RAILWAYS RECORDS: BR/PER(S)34/113

One of the most noticeable changes in everyday British life during the war was the number of women entering many kinds of jobs for the first time, thousands of whom worked in the munitions factories. It has been estimated that about 60% of workers making shells were women.

27 These two pages come from a Report on the Health of Munitions Workers, especially in relation to the employment of women. It was addressed to David Lloyd George who became Minister of Munitions in the Coalition Government in May 1915.

RECORDS OF THE SCOTTISH HOME AND HEALTH DEPARTMENT: HH 31/27/1

Health of Munition Workers Committee.

MEMORANDUM No. 4.

EMPLOYMENT OF WOMEN.

To the Right Honourable
DAVID LLOYD GEORGE,
Minister of Munitions.

Sir,

1. Though some brief reference has already been made in other memoranda issued by the Committee to certain matters affecting the employment of women, there are substantial grounds for dealing in a single memorandum with the various and difficult problems involved. It will be generally admitted that in considering the conditions of employment of women workers as compared with those of men, account must be taken not only of physiological differences but also of those contributions which women alone can make to the welfare of the State. Upon the womanhood of the country most largely rests the privilege of creating and maintaining a wholesome family life and of developing the higher influences of social life. In modern times, however, many of the ideals of womanhood have found outward expression in industry and in recent years hundreds and thousands of women have secured employment within the factory system. The problems thus raised are numerous, but broadly they may be considered as chiefly concerned with the wise and effective organisation of women's industry, in such a way as to protect and safeguard their unique contribution to the State.

2. The engagement of women in the manufacture of munitions presents many features of outstanding interest. Probably the most striking is the universal character of their response to the country's call for their help ; but of equal social and industrial significance is the extension of the employment of married women, the extension of the employment of young girls, and the revival of the employment of women at night. The munition workers of to-day include dressmakers, laundry workers, textile workers, domestic servants, clerical workers, shop assistants, University and Art students, women and girls of every social grade and of no previous wage-earning experience ; also, in large numbers, wives and widows of soldiers, many married women who had retired altogether from industrial life, and many again who had never entered it. In the character of the response lies largely the secret of its industrial success, which is remarkable. The fact that women and girls of all types and ages have pressed and are pressing into industry shows a spirit of patriotism which is as finely maintained as it was quickly shown. Conditions of work are accepted without question and without complaint which, immediately detrimental to output, would, if continued, be ultimately disastrous to health. It is for the nation to safeguard the devotion of its workers by its foresight and watchfulness lest irreparable harm be done to body and mind both in this generation and the next.

3. More than ever in the past should consideration now be given to the well-being of young girls fresh from school, of the prospective mother, and of the mother whose care is especially claimed by her infant during the first months of its life ; for more than ever is their welfare of importance to the State, and much more than ordinarily is it threatened by conditions of employment.

Speaking generally, there are five matters, which apart from questions of wages, concern the health and industrial output of the worker, and which demand the careful attention of employers in regard to the employment of women on any large scale, viz.: (1) the period of employment (including night-work, length of hours, overtime, &c.); (2) rest pauses and the provision of meals ; (3) sanitary conditions of the factory ; (4) physical condition of women workers ; (5) questions of management and supervision. The Committee recognise that certain collateral issues, such as housing, transit and the means of recreation are also intimately concerned in the welfare of women workers, although they may lie somewhat outside the immediate sphere of the employer. The Committee have given careful consideration to the subjects enumerated above, and they desire to offer some observations under each heading. They appreciate the exceptional importance of women's labour in the present emergency, and they do not desire to suggest the imposition of conditions which are likely to embarrass employers or restrict the usefulness

(B 5249)   A 2

of women. They confine themselves, therefore, to matters which in their view are both necessary and urgent in the interest of the women themselves, and the industrial output of which they are capable.

I.—Periods of Employment.

4. *Night Work.*—The imperative necessity of war has revived, after almost a century of disuse, the night employment of women in factories. Prohibited for the textile trades by the factory legislation of 1844, it disappeared gradually in Great Britain, and also in other countries, until, after inquiry and deliberation, it was banished by international agreement from the twelve European countries which signed the Convention drawn up at the International Conference held at Berne in 1906.* These countries included Great Britain, Austria, Belgium, France, Germany, Italy, Portugal, Switzerland and Spain. The agreement was based upon the results of inquiries into the effects, economical, physical, and moral, of night work for women. The reports showed deterioration in health caused by the difficulty of securing sufficient rest by day ; disturbance of home life with its injurious effects upon the children ; and diminished value of the work done—the common experience being that night work was inferior to day work. Now once more all these half-forgotten facts are in evidence in the Munition Factories. In a working-class home the difficulty in obtaining rest by day is great ; quiet cannot be easily secured ; and the mother of a family cannot sleep while the claims of children and home are pressing upon her ; the younger unmarried women are tempted to take the daylight hours for amusement or shopping ; moreover, sleep is often interrupted in order that the mid-day meal may be shared. The employment of women at night is, without question, undesirable, yet now it is for a time inevitable ; and the Committee have, therefore, directed their efforts to the consideration of those safeguards which would reduce its risks to a minimum.

5. Evidence is highly conflicting as to the merits of continuous night work as against those of a weekly, fortnightly or monthly change of shift. The Committee have been impressed by the argument that the difficulty of sleeping by day and digesting food by night is largely overcome by practice, and that for this reason it is better to allow women to remain on night shift continuously for some months ; it is also urged with considerable force that only those persons who can make suitable domestic arrangements would engage themselves for continuous night work. On the other hand, it is said that women who are engaged for night work only are disinclined to remain more than a month or two, and that those who offer themselves for permanent night work are less efficient than those who prefer the day shift. The example of the night duty of hospital nurses has been quoted to show that women can work for long periods at night with excellent results. The Committee feel, however, that comparisons cannot be fairly drawn between industrial night work and the night duty of hospital nurses ; not only are nurses a selected and trained body of women, but the disciplined conditions of their life are not those either of the factory or the working-class home. The Committee are fully alive to the disadvantages of a constantly recurring alternation between day and night shifts, but they consider that the matter is one which must be largely dealt with locally on social considerations.

6. It has been stated by some managers and foremen that the last few hours of a twelve-hour night shift yield little output. This greater influence of fatigue at night is partly due to the fact that the hours between 3 a.m. and 6 a.m., and 4 a.m. and 7 a.m. coincide with the period when, apart from industrial fatigue, vitality is low, and partly to the fact that night workers lack the stimulus of a satisfactory meal. There seems little appetite for the meal which occurs between 1 a.m. and 3 a.m., and it is often of a most unsatisfactory character. In one factory visited at night the manager stated that fatigue prevented many of the women from making the effort to go from their work to the mess room though in itself the room was attractive. In another, visited also at night, several women were lying, during the meal hour, beside their piles of heaped-up work ; while others, later, were asleep beside their machines, facts which bear additional witness to the relative failure of these hours. A few women of rare physique withstand the strain sufficiently to maintain a reasonable output, but the flagging effort of the majority is not only unproductive at the moment, it has its influence also upon subsequent output, which suffers as in a vicious circle. The Committee are satisfied, therefore, on the facts before them that the employment of women at night calls for particular care and supervision, and that adequate pauses for rest and meals are indispensable.

7. *House Accommodation and Transit.*—While the urgent necessity for women's work remains, and while the mother's time, and the time of the elder girls, is largely given

* Bulletin of International Labour Office, English edition, Vol. I., 1906, p. 272. Certain minor modifications were inserted by some Powers.

28 A man and woman working together, pressing-on copper bands on shells at the North British Locomotive Company's factory at Glasgow, which undertook munitions manufacture during the war.

BRITISH RAILWAYS RECORDS: BR/LIB(S)5/63

29 Women travellers for the Crawford's Biscuit Company in 1917. The Suffragettes' campaign for the vote for women was called off when war started but in 1918 women's contribution to the war-effort won the vote for those over the age of 30, lowered in 1928 to 21, as for men.

RECORDS OF UNITED BISCUITS LIMITED: GD 381/1/28

30 Objections by the Shop Committee at the Underwood Shell Factory, Paisley, to the way in which the boys from Miss Kibble's Reformatory were being employed in the factory, 1918. The Reformatory itself was equipped to teach the boys various crafts and trades.

This paper was accompanied by a letter (not shown) from the body of adult workers stating that all the details were 'true in every particular', adding:

'We desire to express our sympathy with the boys in their hard lot, and our indignation towards the Directors of the Kibble Institution, who have committed them to it . . . It is, in fact, the merest drudgery, calculated to stifle initiative, stultify intelligence, character and individuality, and encourage those vicious propensities it is the function of a Reformatory to correct. . . . We reject as false, hypocritical, and foolish, the plea of patriotism which is advanced in defence of this unnatural exploitation of youth . . . we are forced to the conclusion that the Kibble boys are being exploited solely to relieve the war-time strain upon the finances of the Kibble Institution.'

RECORDS OF THE SCOTTISH EDUCATION DEPARTMENT: ED 15/73

.1.

Boy Labour in Messrs. Beardmore's

Underwood Shell Works.

Paisley.

From 80 to 90 boys from the Miss Kibble Reformatory are employed in this factory, half the number on day-shift, and half on night-shift. They are marched in military formation to and from the works, accompanied by a warder who remains with them as superviser throughout the day, or night. All the boys are certified to have passed the statutory school-leaving age of fourteen, and those on night-shift to be over sixteen; but so small in stature and so juvenile in appearance are they for the most part that we are sceptical on the point, and suggest inquiry. They are coarsely but comfortably clad, and though their food is of the plainest description, it is possibly nutritious and wholesome enough. This also should be looked into however.

The lads are engaged in general labouring work throughout the factory, chiefly in transporting shell by trolley from the machines to the inspection tables and vice-versa, one of the most laborious jobs, if not indeed actually the heaviest job in the works. A fully loaded truck weighs approximately seven hundredweights.

For the mass of the workers a night-shift comprises 12 hours; toolsetters and Plant engineers work 12½ hours; Kibble boys 13 (7 p.m. to 8 a.m.), they being employed for an hour after the rest of the workers leave in the morning in removing the shell cuttings from the machines in preparation for the incoming shift. This, by the way, is a particularly objectionable task. Similarly on day shift a number of the boys work 10½ hours, and frequently 12½ hours against the rest of the workers 9½

It is generally recognised that nightwork imposes a severe strain even upon adults, so that it is not surprising that these little fellows take advantage of any interval that may occur, (and these intervals are both few and brief) to curl up on their "bogies", on a bench, or on the floor, and snatch forty winks; and that morning finds them in an advanced stage of exhaustion. If our information is correct, however, the Kibble authorities do not scruple on occasion to employ the boys on other manual work during the day between night-shifts, possible recognising that the lads are not in a fit condition for study, and regarding

---

.2.

unoccupied leisure as a waste of time. This should certainly be looked into.

The day-shift squad, we believe, are obliged to spend part of their evenings at their studies.

The boys are paid at the rate of fourpence an hour plus an output bonus. Their average total weekly earnings amount to roughly 22/- day shift, and 31/- on night-shift. Their wages are paid direct to the Institution, and we understand that a proportion of the money is laid aside to the credit of each boy, to be refunded to him when he leaves the Institution on reaching his eighteenth year. Each boy receives sixpence a week pocket-money.

Punishment for certain offences, such as smoking takes the form of a close cropping of the hair if the young delinquent in true prison fashion; an indignity which we have reason to know the boys deeply resent.

We feel bound to testify that we have found the Kibble boys to be, almost without exception, active, intelligent, and obliging; quite up to the standard of the average apprentice.

THE SHOP COMMITTEE.

J. PATON. SECY.

4 NEWS FROM THE BATTLEFIELDS

Letters and parcels, those vital communication lines with normality back home, arrived at the Fronts with incredible regularity, each company's mail bag sent up with the rations. Letters home were often very matter-of-fact not only because the men wished to hide the worst from close relatives and they knew that the letters would be read by the orderly officer, but also because a great many soldiers were not accustomed to putting their thoughts and feelings on paper. Postcards were the normal way of acknowledging parcels. By 1918 the Army Postal Service was employing 4,000 soldiers to handle the mail, while its parcels section occupied a five-acre wooden building in Regent's Park, London.

31 Soldiers snatch a brief rest in a trench on the Western Front; one of them is writing a letter.

32 Part of an Official Report on the part played by the 9th Lancers in the action at Moncel and Provins.

21 September 1914.

'We have had a terrible week in this past battle, manning the trenches by night and day alongside the Guards and digging like mad, my word, we have had a shelling. Yesterday we were moved to the right of the English line, the Second Cavalry Brigade re-occupying the trenches that had been evacuated, driving the Germans out, and holding them till the arrival of fresh troops, I think the biggest thing this Brigade has done.

Fraser and Mardon were both wounded. Today we are having a real rest and refit, and by Jove, we wanted it. We have got I am glad to say our greatcoats back, but nothing else, and they say everything we sent from Tournay to the Base was either burnt or sent to Southampton. It is getting very cold, and has rained incessantly for a week. This great battle has now lasted eight days, I wonder how many more! The discomfort is awful. For the last week the Germans have mounted huge guns, that fire 90lbs melinite shells that make an appalling noise and if they hit anything do enormous damage, their explosion is deafening. We must have had some 500 over us yesterday, I know my head fairly ached.'

SEAFORTH MUNIMENTS: GD 46/6/127

33 The Rev. Robert J. Thomson, minister of Coldstream, serving with the First Battalion, Black Watch Regiment, to Lady Clementine Waring, from Flanders.

22 October 1915.

'My first Sunday in the trenches was memorable. No sound of church bell, not even an Angelus* trembled across the land — nothing but the everlasting whizz of bullets and the shriek of shrapnel . . . The sun shone beautifully, but on what a sight! The ugliest of German barbed wire rusted with the blood of heroes; two dead bodies entangled therein, their faces masked in hideous smoke helmets. There were two redeeming points in the landscape — two that reminded us of something other than the brutality of war. Two red poppies grew out of the side of the parapet, while a church spire was silhouetted against a golden sky away in the South. I felt like plucking the poppies and planting them beside the corpses among the wire. What could have been more symbolical and fitting! The "flower of dreams", as Francis Thompson calls the poppy.

I have been appointed bombing officer for the battalion, and go on a course of instruction next week. I smile to myself when I think of the minister of Coldstream as bombing officer for the 42nd . . . However, I'll do my best to show that an old tea-drinking, drawing room, effeminate preaching parson can do something to substantiate his religion!!!'

*bell for prayer.

WARING OF LENNEL PAPERS: GD 372/87/12

34 An officer on the Western Front to Lady Clementine Waring, 1915 or 1916.

'After wandering up the communication trench I got into the firing line and there the sight was awful. Wounded men and dead men lay in the bottom of the trench and on the parapet with the ghastly wire entanglements just beyond. This was my very first visit to the very front line and I think I had a weird introduction. I came across a wounded officer lying in a little sap running out of the trench. I was told it was Mister Home, one of the officers of my Company. He had been brought in over the parapet by one of the men. I bent down and asked him how he was and he told me he was all right but felt cold. (As a matter of fact he was wounded in the right thigh and left leg). I threw my great coat over him and told him to buck up, as the stretcher-bearers would be along soon...A little further I found a young lad whom I knew at Nigg. He had been in the same Company as I was in there, when a private. He was groaning badly being wounded in the back. He asked me for a drink of water but my bottle was empty and as he was bleeding I did not wish to give him any of the whisky out of my flask. So I only moistened his lips with alcohol and passed on — but not before he had recognised me. The next wounded man I came to was evidently in excessive pain so I stopped to give him a couple of morphine tabloids . . .

For a short time I was standing close by the machine gun . . . Alongside the Gun there reclined a wounded man. The gunner . . . told him to put his finger on the trigger and let off a shot to repay the Bosche who had hit him. But the man was too sore so the gunner [took] hold of his hand and pressed his finger on the trigger letting off a shot. Both men smiled and were greatly pleased with themselves.

It is astonishing to see how these fellows help one another. They are full of kindness, tenderness and self-sacrifice . . . Their bright spirits under such trying circumstances would amaze you; and their courage is magnificent. I tell you they are a splendid set of fellows and men to be proud of.'

WARING OF LENNEL PAPERS: GD 372/99/44

35 From the diary of an officer in the Dardanelles campaign, describing the evacuation.

January 1916.

'January 1. H.Q. in the morning when we were told Helles was to be evacuated almost at once ... This was a great relief as the place is getting most unhealthy.

January 5 ... Just after lunch I got a message from "C" Coy to say that a shell had burst in the Crater killing Evans and three men and wounding several — most unfortunate. I had been talking to Evans only about an hour before ... There was rather heavy shelling by both sides from 4.00 to 5.00, the Turks shelled our trenches chiefly with "whizz-bangs", so-called — you don't hear them coming they come so fast! We had one man, a sentry killed.

January 8. Our last day! by daybreak all the troops were in their final positions — everything was normal — we had nothing to do beyond destroying anything of any use that was left lying about and marking out with flour the track to follow ... The first party to leave started off at 4.25 — 120 all ranks — then we had to wait till dark ... We did not actually move off till 8.10 — everything quiet. The Turks fired 3 shells over the Gully as we went down ... We got down to Gully Beach without mishap at 9.15 ... We were marshalled in parties of 400 or near ... One looked anxiously at the sea all the way, the wind increasing all the time! It took nearly an hour to get to "W" Beach and then we had to wait our turn for a lighter, finally getting aboard about 11.00. We had no distance to be taken and ran alongside a destroyer HMS Lawford and transhipped to her.

The Officers were most hospitable and gave us most excellent cocoa and biscuits. They took nearly 1300 men on board ...

January 9. We got to Imbros about 4.30 and went alongside the flagship HMS Lord Nelson and got everybody aboard her. We had an excellent breakfast, everything so clean! ... did not get to Mudros till 3.30. Here we disembarked and marched to our former camp ... In the morning we heard everyone was off with practically no casualties ... It was a great relief to get one's boots off and lie down with the feeling that one need not get up till one wanted to ...'

HAY OF BELTON MUNIMENTS: GD 73/2/26

36 The evacuation of the Dardanelles: soldiers on a raft with a gun, making for a transport ship.

THE ILLUSTRATED LONDON NEWS: BRITISH RAILWAYS RECORDS: BR/PER(S)34/114

37 Frank Ward of the B.E.F. in France to the Countess of Buckinghamshire, thanking her for a parcel.

21 June 1916.

'My Lady
I received the parcel which you so kindly sent out to me last night and the contents were quite safe and not damaged. I may say it was a very nice surprise and also a nice feed, as at present we are away from any place where we might buy extras. Our Batt. has been in the line for about a week we then came out for a rest and are now expecting to go up again shortly. I may say it is not a very pleasant place to be in yet I shall be glad to get in the line again as where we are now staying is so quiet and dull. I will now close, thanking you very much indeed for the parcel.'

I remain
your obedient servant
Frank Ward.
Reg. No. 2970, 12 Platoon,
C Coy, B.E.F. France.

FORDELL MUNIMENTS: GD 172/1319/1

38 Postcards from prisoners of war in Germany, the Gordon Highlanders Regiment, acknowledging parcels sent to them through the Prisoners of War Bureau, Aberdeen. 1916.

GRANT OF MONYMUSK MUNIMENTS: GD 345/1418

POST CARD.

Colonel Grant.

THE HON. SECRETARIES,

PRISONERS OF WAR BUREAU

COUNTY BUILDINGS,

ABERDEEN,

SCOTLAND.

FOR ACKNOWLEDGMENT OF PARCEL.

ex GD345/1418

Please quote:—

Reg'tl No. 3040   Regiment 5ᵗʰ Gordon Highlanders

Barrack   Camp Schneidemühi,

Date of Receipt 30ᵗʰ Oct.

I have to acknowledge receipt of parcel (or parcels) dated 16ᵗʰ Aug. 13ᵗʰ Sept. containing cakes syrup. butter. tea. sugar. milk. salmon. paste. fruit. soap.

Signed Fred M Kindness

POSTCARD.

THE HON. SECRETARIES,

PRISONERS OF WAR BUREAU,

COUNTY BUILDINGS,

ABERDEEN,

SCOTLAND.

FOR ACKNOWLEDGMENT OF PARCEL.

ex GD345/1418

Please quote:—

Reg'tl No. 1416   Regiment 5ᵗʰ Gordon High.

Barrack Block 2   Camp bg g   Minden

Date of Receipt 11ᵗʰ Nov.

I have to acknowledge receipt of parcel (or parcels) dated 13ᵗʰ Oct containing Tin Meat Biscuits Butter & Sugar Soap Fish Milk Jam ect

Signed R S Anderson

Feldpostkarte.

Colonel Grant

Monymusk

Aberdenshire

Scotland

ex GD345/1418

August 27/9/16

Dear Sir

I have received your kind and welcome Parcel you sent me on the 28 June and I thank you with the highest of respects for it, it came at the night time for I had nothing and it was a great help to m hopping this will find you in good health

Your truly Friend A Crawford good night

39 Miss Sarah Macnaughtan serving as a nurse in Russia, to Lady Clementine Waring, from Petrograd.

[12 November 1916].

'The distress amongst the Refugees in Russia is quite awful. Some of them are still tramping from Poland after the first battles there, others are hiding in woods, with no shelter or covering, and dying like flies. Officers coming from the Front by rail say that all along the Railway they see these people marching along in families or scooping out holes in the snow in which to shelter . . . The numbers of these poor wretches makes the case so difficult; and still the tales of cruelty go on. How I loathe War! There are 25,000 soldiers in this town alone, with amputated limbs. What earthly use is that, in the name of wonder.'

WARING OF LENNEL PAPERS: GD 372/94/12

40 Polish refugees in flight before the German army, in the autumn of 1915.

THE ILLUSTRATED LONDON NEWS, 28 AUGUST 1915:
BRITISH RAILWAYS RECORDS; BR/PER(S)34/113

Although in the early stages of the war the Trade Union and political Labour movements had accepted various restrictions, such as giving up the right to strike, accepting arbitration over wages and the employment of women and semi-skilled workers in industry in place of those skilled men who had gone to fight, relations between workers and government began to show signs of strain as time went on. This was felt most in those areas of heavy industry which had gone over to the manufacture of munitions where government control of resources and the labour force was strongest.

The situation was intensified by the use of new techniques in engineering and by the rise of the Shop Stewards' movement whose leadership of the work-force was not always in agreement with the attitude of the central Trade Union officials towards co-operation with the government. The Clyde Workers' Committee received most publicity at the time for its militant campaign for 'workers' control' and a number of its members were 'deported' and imprisoned.

UNDERTAKING TO BE SIGNED BY THE CLYDE DEPORTEES.

I (name and address) hereby undertake that if I am permitted by the military authorities to reside in or near Glasgow, I will, while there, remain at work at my trade, provided that suitable work is available, and will, during the continuance of the war, take no part, directly or indirectly, in any stoppage of work or in any action designed to secure a stoppage, or in any other action which is likely in any way to delay or interfere with the manufacture or supply of munitions, or any other work required for the successful prosecution of the war. I undertake further that should I have any grievances which I consider to require redress, I will submit them to be dealt with through the usual constitutional channels by the recognised trade union to which I belong.

a/ 10 August 1916

THE DEPORTED CLYDE STRIKERS.

Mr BARNES (Lab., Glasgow, Blackfriars) asked the Minister of Munitions if he was yet in a position to say if the Clyde deportees were to be allowed to return to their homes, and, if not, what steps could they take to enable them to conform to any reasonable requirement of the Government.

The SECRETARY to the MINISTRY OF MUNITIONS (Dr Addison)—We have received representations in regard to these men both from the Amalgamated Society of Engineers, to which society all or most of the men belong, and from the National Labour Advisory Committee on War Output. We have naturally attached great weight to these representations, and have decided accordingly to permit certain men to return provided that they will accept the employment which will be offered to them there, and are prepared to sign an undertaking embodying, among other matters, a promise to submit any grievance through the recognised machinery of their Trade Union, and to abstain from any act in any way likely to prejudice the supply of munitions or other war work. In coming to this decision as to these particular men, the Minister of Munitions has been guided by a careful examination of records and by the fact that since their removal they have all taken other employment, and, according to our information, have worked loyally up to the present time. In no circumstances can be proceed to deal with the cases of other men for a period of three months, and then only if he is fully satisfied that their conduct has for a substantial period being comparable to that of the men who will now be allowed to return.

Mr BARNES—Does the right hon. gentleman not think that this will only lead to further controversy and trouble, and would it not be better to take the cherry at one bite and make representations to the Minister of Munitions to allow all the men to return?

The SECRETARY to the MINISTRY of MUNITIONS—I cannot undertake to do that. We are watching the matter with the greatest care.

Mr PRINGLE—Who are the men who will not be allowed to return?

The SECRETARY to the MINISTRY of MUNITIONS—The names will be published in a short time.

Mr BARNES—What have these men to do in order to place themselves in a position to comply with the conditions in three months' time?

The SECRETARY to the MINISTRY of MUNITIONS—They have to continue to work quietly and comply with the requirements.

Mr BARNES—Some of them are not at work.

The SECRETARY to the MINISTRY of MUNITIONS—One has refused to work, and therefore we cannot, in any circumstances, allow him to return.

41 Undertaking to be signed by the 'Clyde deportees', if released, August 1916; with newspaper-cuttings of questions in the House of Commons about their release.

RECORDS OF THE SCOTTISH HOME AND HEALTH DEPARTMENT: HH 31/22

'Peace by negotiation' was the slogan of a number of pacifist or near-pacifist organisations whose public meetings were banned whenever possible. Confrontation between these bodies and patriotic citizens led to public disorder on some occasions, while their denunciation of the war and the government's international policies was seen as subversive.

42 Syllabus, for the session 1917-18, of the Glasgow Branch of the Union of Democratic Control.

RECORDS OF THE SCOTTISH HOME AND HEALTH DEPARTMENT: HH 31/19

SYLLABUS

With Short Synopsis of the Ground to be covered by each Lecture

■

General Subject

Internationalism & Militarism

Or, the Practical Application of the Principles of the U.D.C.

■

Introductory.

1917
October 8—" **The Choice before Democracy— Militarism or Internationalism.**"

    Lecturer: **Councillor Egerton P. Wake.**

National isolation impossible—Alternative between World War and World Peace—Progress toward Democracy and internal reform incompatible with periodic war—Effects of periodic war and chronic militarism—Constructive Internationalism—Political organisation of world—How can this be achieved?—Based on Common Will of People—Is the Democracy for War or for Peace?—Even given "will to peace" require organised mediums of understanding, development of international mind, permanent machinery.

Application of First Point.

October 15—" **National and Racial Aspirations of Europe.**"

    Lecturer: **Rev. Raymond V. Holt, B.A., B.Litt.**

Persistence of national principle—Unsatisfied, a menace to peace—Demand for independence: political, economic, cultural—Outstanding European examples—Means of solution and safeguarding—Free Federalism—Protection of League of Nations—Internationalism—Dangers of petty sovereignties—Plebiscite and other methods.

4

October 22—" **Nationalism versus Imperialism: or, Small Nationalities in Relation to Great Empires.**"

    Lecturer: **Mr. George Aitken.**

Causes of Wars—Struggles for independence—Attempts at domination—Rivalries between Great Empires—National idea the key to 19th century movements—Small States of Europe: condition, value, and status — Modern Imperialism — Motives: political, economic, militarist—Charter of Small States—Internationalism complement of nationalism.

Application of Second Point.

November 5—" **Historical Resumé of European Alliances and Treaties.**"

    Lecturer: **Mr. James B. Houston, M.A.**

The Holy Alliance—Concert of Europe—Dual and Triple Alliance—Triple Entente—Balkan League—Treaties: variety of kinds—Example of secret treaties or clauses—Binding power and sanctity of treaties—Treaties, kept and broken—Some celebrated Treaties, 1800-1914.

November 12—" **Machinery of Diplomacy— Bureaucratic versus Democratic.**"

    Lecturer: **Rev. Campbell Stephen, B.D., B.Sc.**

Diplomats and Diplomacy of bygone times—Birth of modern diplomacy, 1648—Scant development—Functions of diplomacy—Principles, methods and machinery of present system—Is secrecy essential?—Results of secrecy—Why does Diplomacy fail?—Conceptions of Diplomacy—Suggested reform—Wanted: Power (1) to know; (2) to control—Democratisation of Foreign Office—Parliamentary control—Periodical revision of treaties—Sanctity and sanctions of treaties.

Application of Third Point.

November 19—" **Balance of Power and other Attempts to Secure Peace.**"

    Lecturer: **Mr. John R. Orr, M.A.**

National isolation impossible—Alliances sought—first between units, then groups—Alliances and leagues of the past—Concert of Europe—Holy Alliance—Rise and history of doctrine of Balance of Power—Its definition—Its defects—Historic failures and violations—Opinion by Bright—No longer purely European—The alternative.

5

43 Memo by the Secretary for Scotland for a meeting of the War Cabinet, on the proposed prohibition of a meeting of the Workers' and Soldiers' Council in Glasgow, 6 August 1917.

RECORDS OF THE SCOTTISH HOME AND HEALTH DEPARTMENT: HH 31/19

SECRET.

G.T.1625   WAR CABINET.   37

PROPOSED PROHIBITION OF A MEETING AT GLASGOW.

Memorandum by the Secretary for Scotland.

The Chief Constable of Glasgow has reported to the Magistrates' Committee of that city that it is proposed to hold a meeting of the Workers' and Soldiers' Council in Glasgow at 3 p.m. on Saturday next, 11th inst., The notice calling the meeting is issued by the "Provisional Committee of the Workers' and Soldiers' "Council", who state that they have divided the United Kingdom into thirteen districts and are arranging for a conference in each district. A Conference for the whole of Scotland is to be held on the date above mentioned. Proposed resolutions include one to the effect that "this conference, endorsing the resolutions of the "Leeds Convention, hails the Russian Revolution........ and under- "takes to work for an agreement between the international democra- "cies for the re-establishment of a general peace which shall not "tend towards either domination by or over any nation, or the "seizure of their national possessions, or the violent usurpation "of their territories, a peace without annexations or indemnities.... "Further, calls on the Government of Great Britain to place itself "in accord with the democracy of Russia by proclaiming its deter- "mination to carry into immediate effect a charter of liberties "establishing equal political and social rights for all men and "women".

A further resolution is to be proposed that "this conference "pledges itself to work............for the full application of "the programme outlined in the fourth resolution of the Leeds "Convention........Further, demands from the Government for all "soldiers immediately the right of association and full civil and "political liberty. To that end...........calls upon the "bodies represented at once to establish Workers' and Soldiers' "Councils in their own localities /

....

- 2 -

"..... suggests that, wherever possible, the Trades "Council should take the initiative."

The Secretary for the Glasgow district is Mr. William Shaw, Secretary, Glasgow Trades Council. The Provisional Committee include George Lansbury, J.Ramsay Macdonald, Tom Quelch, Robert Smillie, Philip Snowden, W.C. Anderson, F.W. Jowett, etc.

The Magistrates, on receipt of the Chief Constable's recommendation, held a meeting, which the Lord Provost and the Sheriff of Lanarkshire also attended, and as the result the Town Clerk, with the concurrence of all those authorities, was instructed to ask the Secretary for Scotland to authorise the Lord Provost and the Chief Constable jointly, in terms of Regulation 9A of the Defence of the Realm Regulations, to issue an Order prohibiting the holding of the proposed meeting. The reasons prompting the request are summarised in a telegram received from the Town Clerk, to the effect that "there is apprehension of grave "disorder arising because of disturbances at previous "meetings of similar character in Glasgow, and of "disturbances in other towns arising out of meetings of the "Workers' and Soldiers' Councils. A counter demonstration "has been threatened, if the meeting is allowed to proceed. "At least 200 police would require to be specially allocated "to afford protection and prevent disorder, and this, in "view of the large reduction, amounting to nearly one "half of the available police force, would be an undue "demand. The holding of the meeting on a Saturday "afternoon, when the streets are crowded and all the "police are required for ordinary duty throughout the "city, greatly adds to the difficulty. At a meeting "held in Charing Cross Halls. Glasgow, on 12th April, "addressed by Mr. Ramsay Macdonald, disorder actually "occurred, and the presence of a large body of police "was required to restore and maintain order." The

Chief

44 Part of a speech by the Prime Minister, David Lloyd George, underlining the importance of the Press in keeping up national morale.
14 July 1917.

'During the forthcoming critical phase of the war, the government feel that it is necessary for it to keep in touch with the Press of the whole country. To begin with the contact between the Press and the political leaders is far less close than in times of peace. On the other hand, the Government is far too busy with war work to do the necessary public speaking all over the country. The ordinary methods of educating public opinion are greatly diminished because so much of the ordinary political life of the community is in abeyance. Therefore, an enormous responsibility rests upon the Press . . . on the one hand to give publicity to the views of the people . . . On the other hand they have to lead and direct the people and prevent them from being mislead or rattled by propaganda or in times of crisis . . .

Criticism is the life blood of public life. But to be valuable that criticism must be based upon real knowledge of the situation. Government think an occasional conference at which situations be explained more fully than is possible in public would be of general advantage not only to the Press but to the country.

The really trying time is now approaching — the autumn and winter. It is a time during which morale may be more decisive than guns and armies. Every attempt will be made by German manoeuvres, assisted by blind pacifist revolutionary forces, to divide the Allies and rattle and divide the nation. It is the last hope of victory for the German machine . . . It is up to the Press to see that National morale is kept up and that our Allies and the Dominions continue to feel that we are still the steady leaders of the war against Prussian autocratic power.

Victory is certain — if we pull together and every man and woman does his bit. But the war is not yet won . . . The power of the Press may be decisive. They have it in their power to win or lose the War.'

LOTHIAN MUNIMENTS: GD 40/17/641/2

45 Mr David Lloyd George, The British Prime Minister (right) with General Haig (left), commander of the British troops, and General Joffre (centre), commander of the French. The figure on the far left has not been identified.

By 1917 a certain disillusion with the war had set in, partly encouraged by the tales told by soldiers on leave of conditions in the battlefields, by the news of the appalling numbers of casualties on the Fronts and by the increased hardship at home through restrictions and shortages and the fear of air raids. The civilian mood of patriotism and romantic hero-worship of the earlier years gave way to a realistic effort to see the business through to a victorious finish for the Allied forces.

The Military Service Bill, passed in January 1916, introduced conscription giving the government power to enlist all single men aged between 18 and 41. The following May the Universal Conscription Act made all males between 18 and 41 liable for service. Tribunals were set up to hear appeals from those who wished to claim exemption, on grounds of employment in essential work or through 'conscientious objection', for religious or political reasons, to killing one's fellow men.

The 'Conchies', as the conscientious objectors were called, were extremely unpopular with those who had lost relatives in the war and they were pilloried in propaganda.

46 A 'conscience' poster, probably the best-known from the First World War.

Daddy, what did YOU do in the Great War?

47 Part of a letter to the Prime Minister in 1917 from Reginald Clifford Allen, later Baron Allen of Hurtwood, of the 'No Conscription Fellowship', while imprisoned as a conscientious objector, in which he explains his point of view and complains of the humiliating treatment by the authorities of himself and fellow-prisoners.

LOTHIAN MUNIMENTS: GD 40/17/518/2

The Cells,

No.4 Parkhouse Camp,

Salisbury Plain.

31st May 1917.

Dear Mr. Lloyd George,

I have to-day been paraded before the troops here and received my third successive sentence of imprisonment with Hard Labour. This time my sentence is for two years.

Before I am removed to prison I think it right to make known to you that, like other men similarly situated, I have recently felt it my duty to consider carefully whether I ought not for the future to refuse all orders to work during imprisonment. I have decided that it is my duty to take this course. This will mean that I shall be subjected to severe additional punishments behind prison doors. Provided I have the courage and health to fulfil this intention, I shall have to spend the whole of my sentence in strict solitary confinement in a cell containing no article of any kind - not even a printed regulation. I shall have to rest content with the floor, the ceiling and the bare walls. I shall have nothing to read and shall not be allowed to write or receive letters or visits, and shall live for long periods on bread and water.

I am anxious you should understand that I have not arrived at this decision from any lust for martyrdom. Hitherto I have

exercised all my influence with Conscientious Objectors to persuade them to fulfil all prison obligations, but I feel it would be wrong for me to do so any longer, and I beg you to allow me to tell you why.

You, like so many people, have always looked upon us men as either cowards or stupid enough to have a mania for martyrdom. You consider us cowards in that we are at any rate safer and better off in prison than in the trenches. And yet you are perfectly well aware that our choice has not been, and is not, between prison and the trenches. That is not why we are in prison. Before the Tribunals many of us were offered as a condition of exemption an opportunity of finding ordinary civil work in which we should have been free to live our everyday lives, exempted from every kind of military service. We refused the offer, claiming Absolute Exemption.

Then the Government, which included yourself, punished us for this by arresting us and sending us to be soldiers, although we had already proved to the entire satisfaction of the Tribunals that we had a genuine objection to every kind of military service. Naturally we refused to be soldiers and were then (following in some cases upon a spasm of brutal treatment) packed off to prison for disobedience to military orders.

Next you offered to release us from prison not on condition that we would go to the trenches, but provided we would sign an agreement to engage in safe civil work with other men similarly minded to ourselves. We were to be nominally transferred to Army Reserve W., and if we misbehaved, we should be sent back to our regiments. A recent stipulation has been that those who accept this work should not engage in the public

propaganda of their opinions. Again we refused this ostensibly attractive offer and chose to remain in prison at Hard Labour.

Then you sent us back to the Army, and we were again court-martialled and again imprisoned, and now, like many others, after being returned to the Army, and sentenced again, I am to be sent back to prison with Hard Labour for the third time - and so, I suppose, ad infinitum.

I think this shows that - mad or sane - we are at least not cowards. It is not the fear of physical death in the trenches that has led to our remaining in prison, but rather a fear of spiritual death which we believe must follow our assent to any Conscription Scheme, military or civil.

If then we are not cowards, it is argued that we must like playing the martyr. On the contrary, we have chosen to remain in prison rather than accept all those attractive offers, because we cannot honestly accept anything but Absolute Exemption from a Military Service Act, - a form of exemption provided for in the Act and actually granted to some 400 Conscientious Objectors.

When we say we can only accept Absolute Exemption, we mean this. As proved and admitted genuine Conscientious Objectors (which we are by the statutory Tribunals) we believe war to be wrong. Thus we believe the same of Militarism, and thus we believe the same of Conscription, which is designed to equip the nation in its military and civil spheres for war. And so we say nothing in the world will induce us to accept any compromise or enter into any bargain with a Conscription Act.

Our repeated refusal of all these offers does not, however, signify unwillingness to render life service either to our fellow-

- 2 -

- 3 -

48 The first Christmas Eve in the trenches, 1914. A war artist's impression of the spontaneous truce between soldiers of both sides when drink, food, cigarettes and even photographs and addresses were exchanged. These short, impromptu truces, which occurred at intervals during the war, were sternly dealt with by the High Command.

THE ILLUSTRATED LONDON NEWS, 9 JANUARY 1915:
BRITISH RAILWAYS RECORDS, BR/PER(S)34/113

49 Towards the end of the war, in September 1918, a friend wrote from the Eastern Front to Lady Clementine Waring:

'You must all at home, as we are here, be feeling so very much more cheerful these days than you (and we) have been during the early months of the summer — in consequence of the almost too wonderful news which we are getting now — ... the magnificent success of the Palestine show with its colossal hauls of prisoners which increase in thousands per day and materials such as we know not what to do with ...

Macedonia is also the scene of routs and captures and advances in large strides and Bulgaria wavers and totters and shreiks* for mercy ... but thank God we have after 4 years become a little hard, a little vengeful and the upper lip of us has stiffened and purpose hardened.'

*spelt thus in original

WARING OF LENNEL PAPERS: GD 372/87/3

6 LAND, SEA AND AIR

50 A fragile record from the battlefield: relief orders in the trenches, 1 May 1917, giving instructions about taking over positions and equipment, notably the Lewis guns. Local landmarks, such as 'the Orchard' and the 'Railway Embankment' are mentioned. The orders conclude, 'Rations for the Coy will be dumped in the trench to be occupied and will be found there on arrival.'

MISCELLANEOUS COLLECTIONS: GD 1/731/1

51 Canadian troops 'going over the top' of a trench at the start of an attack.

52 Notes on the German submarine campaign by J.E. Masterton Smith, the Admiralty, sent to Philip Kerr, secretary to the Prime Minister, David Lloyd George, 29 January 1917, summarised the effects of U-boat operations:

53 Photograph of a German U-Boat. At one point in 1917, when due to submarine attacks on merchant shipping there were only six weeks' imported food supplies left in Britain, it looked as if the British Isles might be starved into surrendering.

'... I tell you plainly that the scale and scope of the German submarine attacks upon the merchant shipping, not only of ourselves and of our Allies, but of the whole world, constitute a very serious danger. The surface supremacy of the sea is, and has been, ours since the beginning of the war. It has scarcely even been challenged ...

But the barbarous, ruthless nature of the underwater war upon peaceful shipping is another story. Like all new dangers it must be met — and is being met — by new methods ...

We have got to tackle ... the problem at both ends. At one end we have got to destroy as many enemy submarines as we can ... I do not believe the British Navy will fail us now: they have never failed us yet.

At the other end we are adopting what I may call defensive measures: and here I mean the vigorous efforts the Government are making to economise tonnage, to restrict superflous imports, to provide British merchant vessels with a defensive armament, and to build new ships ... I often wonder how long neutrals will endure the ruthless sinking of their ships without giving their own merchant seamen the same measure of protection which for centuries has been recognised as the right of all who sail the broad seas.

As to construction of ships, our aim is to see that if possible as many ships are put into the pool as the Germans can take out of it. The Shipping Controller, in conjunction with the Admiralty, is hard at work laying down fresh keels. What we want is a standardized cargo vessel — a sort of "Ford" merchant ship — whose parts can be built and put together with great speed.'

54 Women at work in a naval shipbuilding yard during the war.

THE ILLUSTRATED LONDON NEWS, 10 JUNE 1916:
BRITISH RAILWAYS RECORDS: BR/PER(S)34/114

MEMORANDUM ON
AIR POWER v. MAN POWER.

The Necessity for Concentration and Unification of the Air Services.

The longer the war goes on the more important, relatively and actually, the air services become. Originally, in the opinion of most Naval and Military officials, the air services were not destined to play anything but a subsidiary part in operations by sea and land. Any idea that aircraft would be employed by the British, French and German forces on the present scale would have been laughed at. In the near future much greater numbers of aircraft will be used. Thus, while the man power of each nation is declining, and will decline, air power will increase, and it is probable that before the end of the war the rest of the arms, including artillery, infantry and cavalry, may take a less important part in offensive operations than the air services. Assuming that this state of things may come to pass before long, we must consider:

1. Whether the present system of administration, organisation, and use of the two air services is applicable to the very much altered and extended character of their operations in the future.

2. Whether the time has not now arrived when all the different forms of the air services should be amalgamated and a united air service established on a separate and independent basis with its own organisation and power to initiate independent offensive operations, though continuing to work as at present in harmony with the Navy and Army.

There is sure to be a great deal of opposition to any suggestion that an amalgamation of the two air

- 1 -

services should take place, for it must be remembered that from the inception of naval and military aviation to the present time most senior officers of the Navy and Army have always looked upon the Flying Services as subsidiary and ancillary to the two older services. Most officers in supreme command by sea and land still consider that sea and air planes should be kept solely for use with their particular forces and they consider them merely as a useful part of their general forces, in the same way that destroyers are useful to and part of a Fleet and artillery of the Army. Thus, it is clear that the idea of the independence of and separate action by the air services will probably be opposed by the older and less progressive officials at both the Admiralty and War Office, especially at the former. Indeed, at the Admiralty there has been from the beginning a distinctly unsympathetic attitude on the part of the higher officials towards the R.N.A.S., both with regard to the lighter than air and heavier than air sections. This attitude has recently been modified, though it exists in some quarters still. One instance out of many of the casual way in which air questions were considered is found in the fact that only in May of this year was an official seaplane carrier laid down for delivery in about a year's time. In other words, it will be nearly four years after the beginning of war before the first properly designed naval airplane carrier is available, other ships not really suitable having been used up to now.

In regard to the War Office, the treatment of the air service began to be more sympathetic at an earlier date, but this was chiefly due to the fact that the work of the R.F.C. soon became so absolutely necessary to the conduct of operations in the field by Army and Corps commanders that its importance had

to be recognised. To-day artillery commanders would be unable to carry out their duties efficiently without the use of airplanes to give them information and advise them as to results of bombardment.

This control of the Flying Services by the Navy and Army has naturally led to raids not being attempted on a really large scale, for the anxiety of Admirals and Generals is to keep their flying machines for operations with their units rather than allow any independent offensive to be undertaken except near their own lines.

- 2 -

56 One of the aircraft exhibited around Scotland during 'war weapons week' in 1917, when towns and villages were encouraged to save for tanks and aeroplanes: this one, which carries the name of Inverarity, Angus, is an S.E.5a, rival of the Sopwith Camel for the title of the most successful British fighter of the First World War.

RECORDS OF THE NATIONAL SAVINGS COMMITTEE: NSC 1/393

NOTES ON THE USE OF CARRIER PIGEONS.

USE OF CARRIER PIGEONS.

During the recent operations, Carrier Pigeons have proved of great value for purposes of communication and have in many cases brought in most important information through a heavy barrage of Artillery fire and through Gas clouds when no other means of communication was practicable.

This means of communication is capable of further development, but to obtain full value from it, the principles of the use of this service and the care of the birds must be thoroughly understood by all concerned. The following notes on the subject are therefore issued for guidance :—

ORGANISATION OF THE CARRIER PIGEON SERVICE.

1. The service consists of "Lofts" (Stationary, Motor Mobile, Horse Drawn Mobile) and "Pigeon Stations" (with Infantry) and "Mobile Pigeon Stations" (with Cavalry Divisions).

The Lofts are where the Pigeons are normally kept and to which they home, the Stations are the points to which birds are taken and whence they are released, with messages, as required.

2. All Lofts are under the Director of Army Signals, General Headquarters, who is responsible for the provision of Lofts at suitable places, for the provision and posting of personnel to the Lofts, Stationary or Mobile, and for the supply and maintenance of Pigeons in the Lofts.

As far as possible, all existing Lofts within the area of operations are requisitioned.

Additional Lofts are not to be requisitioned, nor Mobile Lofts or Loft personnel moved without reference to the Director of Army Signals.

Should more Lofts than can be maintained by the G.H.Q. establishment be temporarily required, the necessary personnel will be provided by the Corps concerned, and will be attached as a temporary measure to the G.H.Q. establishment.

The personnel in charge of Lofts will be attached to the nearest Signal unit for administration.

The G.H.Q. establishment is shown in Appendix "A."

3. When a new Loft has to be built and stocked with young birds, it takes six weeks to train the birds before they can be flown from the trenches.

In the case of Mobile Lofts it takes a week for the birds to settle down after the Loft is established in a new position. In addition birds should be trained for a further week on the new line they will have to fly. It will thus take about a fortnight from the time the Loft is moved before the birds are fit to fly from the trenches.

4. In each Cavalry Division four Pigeon Stations will be maintained and attached to the Divisional Signal Squadron.

The establishment for these four Pigeon Stations is shown in Appendix "B."

Cavalry Divisions will have a Loft or share of a Loft allotted to them, when required, by the formation under whom they are working.

5. In each Army in addition to a small establishment attached to the Headquarters of the Army and each Corps, two Pigeon Stations consisting of three trained men will be attached to each Brigade Section of the Divisional Signal Companies. The Pigeon Service establishment of an Army Headquarters, a Corps Headquarters, and of two Brigade Pigeon Stations is shown in Appendix "C."

6. Armies will inform the Director of Army Signals what Lofts they require allotted to Corps.

Training of the young birds in the Lofts will be carried out by the Corps concerned.

A.D.A. Signals of a Corps will be responsible for :

(a) Keeping Army H.Q. informed as to what Lofts are required or may be required in his area. The time required for the establishment of new Lofts, as indicated in paragraph 3 above, must be borne in mind ;

(b) Deciding from which Lofts Divisions are to draw their Pigeons ;

(c) Drawing the equipment shown in Appendix "C" and distributing it to the Lofts and to Divisional Signal Companies as required.

In deciding the distribution of the Pigeons to the various Pigeon Stations in the Corps, the following principles must be observed :—

For continuous work it is necessary to provide at least three times as many Pigeons as it is desired to keep in the trenches at any one time. This will allow for casualties and for the birds to have at least two days in their Lofts for every two days in the trenches. Thus, for a Pigeon Station which is to have four birds constantly in the front line, the Corps must allot at least 12 birds.

For short periods of special pressure, this proportion of rest may be decreased, but if it is decreased for any length of time the birds will suffer.

The amount of equipment, baskets, books, message carriers, etc., is calculated on a basis of two Pigeon Stations per Infantry Brigade, so that the number of Pigeon Stations in a Corps must not exceed twice the number of Brigades in the Corps.

7. Three trained Pigeon men are allowed for each Infantry Brigade Signal Section. These three men are sufficient to man two Pigeon Stations in the Brigade, one man to each Station, and one man to carry full baskets of birds up to the Pigeon Stations and bring back the empty ones.

If more than two Pigeon Stations are required in a Brigade, the personnel for the extra ones must be found by temporarily taking men from Battalions.

It is desirable that six men per Battalion should be trained to handle and fly Carrier Pigeons and so be available to establish these additional Pigeon Stations in a Battalion

---

57 Notes on the use of carrier pigeons, which proved an efficient way of sending messages at the Front. [1916].

HOPE OF CRAIGHALL MUNIMENTS: GD 377/199/24

58 A converted motor-bus being used as a carrier-pigeon 'loft' by the French army, 1915.

THE ILLUSTRATED LONDON NEWS, 2 OCTOBER 1915:
BRITISH RAILWAYS RECORDS, BR/PER(S)34/113

MISCELLANEOUS COLLECTIONS: PAPERS OF THE VERY REV W. WHITE ANDERSON, EDINBURGH. GD 1/625/3

Printed in Scotland for HMSO by (3808), Glasgow.   Dd 287113/HF 4613   C30   10/87